How to Write Clearly

The Meaning Approach

by Ruth Beechick

**MOTT
MEDIA**
Fenton, Michgian

ISBN10: 0-88062-074-9
ISBN13: 978-0-88062-074-1

Contents

Preface

Two conflicting views of English language serve to compli-
cate the lives of all who study it or teach it. In brief nutshell
form, the conflict pits true, historical English on one side against
Latin-driven English on the other side. This book takes the historical English side. The last chapter tells the history of how
English language came to us, and how Latin came to intrude upon
it. This bit of history can sharpen one's understanding and use of
English.

The battle is centuries long. William Cobbett wrote on grammar in 1819, taking the English side, and he clearly saw where
the Latin came from. Because of the long sentences of Cobbett's
time, I have rewritten a paragraph of his, trying to state plainly
all the thoughts it contained.

Why then should we perplex ourselves with numerous
artificial distinctions, which cannot possibly be of any
practical use? Those distinctions came because people
who wrote English Grammars had been taught Latin, and
they were unable to put off the Latin rules. Or they were
unwilling to treat with simplicity that which if it remained
a mystery would make them appear more learned than the
mass of people. Thus they tried to make our simple language turn and twist itself so as to become as complex as
the Latin language is.

One example of Cobbett's criticism of Latin-style grammar
is the conjugations of not just past and present tenses of verbs
but adding I *have worked,* I *had worked,* I *shall have worked,* I
may have worked, and so on. These serve only to fill up a book,
he said. That is not just a conjugation of *to work,* but it introduces

the verb *to have* and its parts. Cobbett cautioned his teenage son against the practice of learning grammar by rote, lest he begin to esteem the powers of memory more than those of reason. A person may retain and repeat a lesson by rote, like a parrot, without any effort of the mind.

With a less sharp pen, Cobbett taught that it is impossible to give precise rules for grammar; much must be left to taste. Dr. Samuel Johnson, H. W. Fowler, and others followed in his train, but we still have not learned the lessons of those past masters. We still think we must pound rules and grammar into students' heads.

Speaking and writing well are essential in our modern civilization. Peter Drucker, leading management expert, expressed it this way.

> The schools teach a great many things of value to the future accountant, the future doctor, the future electrician. Do they also teach anything of value to the future employee? The answer is: "Yes—they teach the one thing that is perhaps most valuable for future employees to know. But few students bother to learn it." This one basic skill is the ability to organize and express ideas in writing and speaking.

Drucker was not an educator, and he blamed the problem on students themselves, whereas Cobbett and others of the past would blame it on our grammar approach to teaching writing. Some educators today agree. S. I. Hayakawa was a professor of English and a university president (before becoming a senator). In the 1900s he wrote a strong message that we might label antigrammar.

> Students trying to express themselves in writing may write poorly. In order to improve their writing, says the

English teacher, I must teach them the fundamentals of grammar, spelling, and punctuation. By thus placing excessive emphasis on grammar and mechanics while ignoring the students' ideas, the teacher quickly destroys student interest in writing. That interest destroyed, the students write even more poorly. Thereupon the teacher redoubles his dose of grammar and mechanics. The students become increasingly bored and rebellious. Such students fill the ranks of "remedial English" classes in high school and college.

A long history of research has shown that grammar is not the route to good writing. The reverse order is more realistic: students should first learn to write acceptably and then study grammar. They can understand it then, and it will provide the vocabulary needed for reading and for discussing grammar and writing. That can begin in the teen years. Before that, students learn a lot of grammar, anyway, but by the meaning approach used in this book. They, of course, must learn the mechanics of punctuation, capitalization, and spelling as they write throughout the elementary school years.

The word *grammar,* in its technical meaning, includes the study of words, their parts of speech, and the study of sentence construction, their syntax. That technical study is what can be delayed until the teen years. With a well organized and condensed list of grammar essentials, students can skim over what they already know, study what they do not know, and finish in probably a month or so. Then that grammar book will serve as a reference and reminder whenever needed.

This book is not set up to drill on the grammar that Cobbett and Hayakawa objected to. Instead, it speaks to writers of any age, from teens on up, focusing on thinking and clear writing, not on rigid rules and grammar. It uses grammar terms as needed, and those are defined briefly in the grammar glossary.

Some examples presented as quotations in this book are not exact quotes, for several reasons. If an author's sentence uses *he* or *they,* I may fill in the people's names so it makes more sense out of its context. If I am illustrating one particular item and a passage distracts with other items, I may delete the distractions to help focus the teaching. So there is no point in citing book and page for such misquotes. The "poor" examples are from student writing and from various publications. If they are from recent magazines, I have imitated them or in other ways disguised them.

The topics and examples explained here show some techniques for analyzing your writing and for analyzing the writing of authors that you read. This kind of study has been shown to improve writing more than do assignments on practicing specific techniques. Writing is for the purpose of communication; above all else it must be clear. And the harder that writers work on clarity the easier it is for their readers. Clarity is a major aim of this book.

1. Message

In this first chapter we look at some "message" aspects of writing. What do you want to say? How will you organize it and say it? Details of sentence formats and word choices come later; first must come the message. In your head.

Pre-planning

Finding your topic. Today's schooling has manufactured the problem of finding topics to write on. A textbook for "composition" class spends a whole chapter on how to come up with topics for a theme each week. That is a problem only because we isolate composition classes from everything else students do. That textbook never suggests finding a topic from history or science class, or current events, or even from literature.

Homeschoolers have a chance to remake the schooling pattern, and some of them do. They may require a report on Napoleon, a summary of *Huckleberry Finn*, or an explanation of DNA molecules. Writing on such topics increases the learning about those topics, because to write, you must think hard, much harder than with just reading or discussing the topics. At the same time, you get writing practice. You must try to organize, write clearly, and use other techniques that this book is about. And after your history or science is done for the day you have no dreaded composition class to face. (Two birds with one stone, to use a cliché.)

Compare that with the trivial textbook suggestions of trying to find a topic by free association scribbling for ten minutes or keeping a private journal, not on your reading or other serious subjects, but just random thoughts. The book suggests teacher assignments too, but many of those seem unnecessary add-ons to busy lives. The topics you need to learn are worth more effort than the topics contrived for the artificial divisions of school classes.

If you are an adult trying to write for blogs or magazines or other publications, you probably have an area of interest that you are writing on, and you already read and think in that area. For everybody, as specific topic ideas hit your brain, you should jot those down before you lose them. One writer says the Bible admonishes him to do that. He should capture the precious thoughts lest they escape and go unused as the meat of a slothful hunter.

> The slothful *man* roasteth not that which he took in hunting: but the substance of a diligent man *is* precious (Proverbs 12:27, KJV).

This jotting of thoughts before you lose them works not only before you begin writing, but it works all through the process. Once your mind is working on a topic, the ideas pop up in bed or in the kitchen or anywhere. They can come while you are reading a different topic. You don't want to get up in the morning and think "Now what was that great idea I had last night?" Capture the precious substance.

You need not always write on school subjects. Sometimes you want to write your own interests or original stories. Do that too. Once you choose a topic, then begins the work of trying to organize it. Several approaches to that job follow.

Beginning to organize. Let's first look at the finished organization of a good writer. He organized with a pie chart showing three equal parts of writing—theory, practice, criticism—and his book carried out that plan. To examine just the third part, criticism, we look at the opening sentences of four paragraphs. These happen to act as topic sentences, so together they form an outline of his message on criticism of writing.

1. For our purposes, criticism is of two types: the objective criticisms [by others] . . . and the subjective criticism that you will apply to your own writing, past and present.
2. The first sort, frankly, will be in short supply. [But take full advantage of it.] . . .
3. The second type of criticism, then—your own ability to diagnose and criticize your own writing—must be stressed constantly. It is a rare ability . . .
4. But rare as the ability may be, it is up to you to develop it . . .

What clear organization we see here! Let's look at it again in shorthand.

1. Criticism is of two types.
2. The first is criticism by others.
3. The second is criticism by self.
4. You must develop the self-criticism.

We do not know of course if the writer had this detailed outline before he began, but it is a good question to ask in general. Most professional writers say no, they cannot outline fully beforehand. They have various starting points and a general idea of where they want to go, but they work out most details during the thinking that accompanies the writing process. And they work out more details as they juggle and reorganize during revisions.

Among novelists, one author says that she needs a detailed outline of what happens in every scene before she can write the novel. That is rare. Other novelists start with interesting characters and write to see what they will do. Still others start with a problem and then write to see how it works out, or they start with a climax and think backward to discover how to get there. In between the extremes are the majority who know the main characters, with their setting and problems, and have a general idea of where the story will go.

School teachers consider outlining to be difficult to teach. It is easier to outline something you read, especially if it is well organized, but usually more difficult to outline something you plan to write. If you can easily outline your report or essay, you probably do not need the outline, as it is already in your head. If making an outline is difficult, then working on one may help. It prods your thinking. Writing plans can be graphics like the pie chart, or any form that helps. They are all types of outlines. Here we look at the traditional schoolbook-style outline.

Outlining. You may need to experiment awhile to see how good an outliner you are. A useful idea is to work at it piecemeal. List the major topics first. Are they parallel? That is, are they of about equal importance? Or are details listed along with larger topics as in this plan?

> 1. Theory of writing
> 2. Practice of writing
> 3. Try to use the help of others

That's not good enough yet, because the items are not equal weight. The first two are big, general topics and the third is one small action to take. Try again.

> 1. Theory of writing
> 2. Practice of writing
> 3. Use the criticism of others, and your own criticism too.

The third is now broader but still not parallel with the others. Change it to "Use criticism." Pretty good. But that is an action and the other two are nouns. Try turning them all to nouns.

> 1. Theory
> 2. Practice
> 3. Criticism

Good. Now set those on paper with space below each for jotting ideas as you think of them. This piecemeal approach works for many people. If you can start from the top of an outline and work your way down in order, then you already have an outline in your head and probably don't need to write one. About three topics, as above, can round out a good essay or article or interesting letter to a friend. You may find that outlining helps with some kinds of writing, such as school assignments. Other times you may begin with a germ of an idea, and your story or essay develops from there.

Sometimes it helps to outline (or repair the original outline) after a project is well along. Outline what you have written and what you still want to write. Move things around on the outline as needed to get them in good order. Juggling on an outline like that is easier then trying to juggle the writing itself. Then the outline can guide as you insert and add and delete to end up with a well organized piece of writing.

An idea germ. A germ that C. S. Lewis started with was a group of images. For *The Lion, the Witch and the Wardrobe*, he described it this way:

> Some people seem to think that I began by asking myself how I could say something about Christianity to children; then fixed on the fairy tale as an instrument . . . then drew up a list of Christian truths and hammered out "allegories" to embody them. This is all pure moonshine. I couldn't write in that way. It all began with images; a faun carrying an umbrella, a queen on a sledge, a magnificent lion. At first there wasn't anything Christian about them; that element pushed itself in of its own accord.

Lewis did not pre-plan the Christian elements or most story elements either. Elsewhere he said elements came out of the furniture of his mind. I also experienced the image route to a story. A high mountain town in Colorado celebrated the hundredth anniversary of an ice palace that miners built back in the pioneer days. An ice palace! Things proceeded from that image out of the furniture of my mind and ended in the book *The Cabin and the Ice Palace.*

Neither *Cabin* nor *Lion* were outlined in detail ahead of time. With non-fiction, too, most authors prefer to work that way, starting with a major idea, and letting elements push themselves in during the writing. There is no single correct formula for planning your next great piece of writing.

Finding your way. Start with an outline? With a germ? With a schoolbook assignment? A writing professor says he is "profoundly suspicious of people who offer a step-by-step system from first idea to published story." He says that recipes work well for cooking and blueprints work for building. But good stories cannot be cooked up or measured out like that; they are not produced by following a rigid set of "rules."

That professor taught fiction, but we could say the same for essays and reports—even paragraphs—any kind of writing. The recipe mode is an occupational hazard of curriculum writers. They want to make the lessons look orderly, not jumbled. One lesson writer worked out an order that began with words. They are the smallest piece of writing, she thought, so the lessons should first teach children a lot of words. Next, came using the words in sentences, and then using the sentences in paragraphs. Fortunately for the children, not many teachers and parents believed in that recipe, so the curriculum fell off the market.

Various other recipes are available, as well as lessons that try their best not to be recipes. You could learn something from just about any of these, but the best learning comes from writing. The motto is: To learn to write, write. Then analyze your writing. That is the most important activity for improving writing.

Read whatever you can on how to write. Discuss with classmates and teacher—or fellow writers. Notice what professional writers do. But most of all write, and then critique your own writing.

The suggestions in this book are some of the things that I have learned along the way. They are not offered as recipes. There are no follow-up assignments to make it look like "this is the way to write." If you want to follow up on one of these ideas, it works best to pull out an already written piece and go over it with that idea in mind. When you are writing something new, you need to focus on the message. You cannot focus at the same time on sentence forms, good word choice, or grammar rules. That work on clarifying and polishing comes during revision, after the first writing.

Writing

After you have some kind of plan, at least a germ, possibly a tentative outline, you can face the paper and begin to write. You know what you want to say, and now come the many decisions about how to say it. This section describes some of those decisions.

A story thread. Two magazine biographical articles differ strikingly because one makes an interesting story of the life while the other almost could have been an encyclopedia article. The encyclopedia article begins in this manner.

John Doehertz was born on June 5, 1861, in Friesberg, in the county of Heatherfield. His father, Karl Doehertz, taught theology at the College of Wemblesite from 1859 to 1864. Then in 1865 he was appointed Professor of Philosophy . . . [More dates and college degrees of John's family members.] John began to study music at Mainz in 1873 . . . [More dates and towns for John's movements.]

The opening three paragraphs contain thirteen dates, and if a reader wants to know how old John was at any event he must do the subtracting himself to determine. If he wants to know if John walked to his music school or if perhaps it was a carriage trip, he needs a good atlas to search out obscure European towns that Americans never heard of and to measure distances. All those interesting "story" elements are missing.

By contrast, the other article dives immediately into the story of the famous person's life.

> Josiah Doe was a great explorer of the 1500s. As a boy growing up he had a dream to sail the untamed seas . . .

That opening led directly into stories of the explorer's experiences. While not full of dates like the other article, it tells more meaningful chronological information. Embedded in the narrative are mentions of how long the trip lasted and other such facts, and readers do not have to do the arithmetic. The only specific date is the start of the explorer's most famous trip.

Do our future writers begin to learn encyclopedia writing in their fifth grade school assignments? If so, the outlook for future reading is bleak.

This story principle applies to other genres besides biographies. Some journalists raise this skill to so high a level that their investigative reports read like novels. We who have not reached that level can nevertheless make all our writing more interesting by realizing that people understand and remember better—and enjoy more—any reading that sounds more like a story than like a list of facts.

Education writers can miss their story by filling pages with abstractions that sound impressively educational. (More on abstractions later.) Here is a sentence from a short paragraph about a pre-school.

> Children are supported in their self expression and problem solving abilities with school projects as well as interpersonal interactions.

With each of those abstractions, readers can fill in whatever comes to mind. Some, by a theory of child psychology they have bought into, could think that children will be allowed *self expression* of their anger; others, again according to their theory of child development, could think of *self expression* via art. *Problem solving abilities* might mean to some that the school teaches arithmetic. And so on. This sort of says something, and the words sound as though that something is good. The rest of the paragraph, too, is filled with words from an *A* student of education: enhanced learning opportunities, optimal learning conditions, engage in academics, stimulating environment, intellectual and emotional needs, socio-emotional skills, cognitive strengths. All this in one four-sentence paragraph. I am tempted to follow that with an exclamation mark, but I'll forego it because of advice I gave elsewhere about not decorating with exclamation marks.

For educators, that abstractionism is easy to write. The hard work would be to buckle down to a more concrete level and describe the "story" of what happens in a classroom, or what will happen with your child if you enroll him, or whatever the writer wishes to focus on. She can then intersperse with higher abstractions to help make the points she is teaching. A constant interplay of high and low level abstractions makes for easy reading and understanding.

Christian "inspirational" writers, too, fill articles with abstract phrases like *the Lord has quickened my understanding* (of what, how), *look to Him for guidance* (how is that done), and *we could see God's hand* over the situation (what was it doing). These sound pious, and experienced Christians can translate or fill in meaning of their own, but they miss the interesting story the writer should have told. I remember when missionary letters all sent the same message—that God was doing great things. But then writers learned to drop the private Christian jargon and tell stories about people, places, and events. So we now learn *what* great things God is doing, and as a bonus we get a good education about what the world is like, a different view than that available in school books and mass media.

Long ago Aristotle wrote of the Greek dramas that they should be complete and unified with a beginning, middle, and end, linked by necessary and probable causes. Good non-fiction, too, should go from somewhere to somewhere and not just wander around in a topic. Sometimes we read an article that wanders and it leaves us wondering what its purpose was. The message was not clear.

Even in catalog blurbs or brief book reviews, writers must find some concrete specifics and tell them clearly. Below, one reviewer seems to think that if he and other important people like the book, and if he can write enough impressive adjectives, then we should buy the book. We don't know whether he is a credible witness or just an aggressive salesman. The other reviewer gives information about the contents of the book so we can decide on that basis whether to read it.

> I was swept away with this splendid book. It is historical writing of the highest order, fascinating in its details, and hailed as a "masterpiece" by . . . This is essential reading for everyone interested in our nation's history . . .

> This archeologist lifts the romanticized veil of sea ice, midnight sun, and flaming auroras to reveal the true Arctic . . . He portrays the movement of Viking farmers across the North Atlantic islands, and the arduous search for a sea route to Asia . . .

Short or long writings—they all need to focus on a message that will interest, inform, or entertain readers.

A good opening. A good opening is difficult to do. Many authors write them last, or at least revise them when the rest of a piece is finished. Dorothy Sayers opened an essay like this.

> I owe a certain debt to Cyrus the Persian. I made his acquaintance fairly early, for he lived between the pages of a children's magazine in a series entitled *Tales from Herodotus*, or something of the kind.

That could be called a dive-in style. It sounds as if she is diving right into a story of what she learned from reading about Cyrus. Then it turns out that Cyrus leads to other historical figures and they lead to still more ideas. This opening, then, is not a statement of the topic but a wedge that widens, leading readers in to the larger message.

If these were topic sentences as taught in old-style schoolbooks, they would say something along the line of Bible people and history people being of the same kind rather than belonging in separate pigeonholes in the brain. The essay opens up still larger ideas of theology. To try to state some of these ideas in topic sentences would place them high on an abstraction ladder, whereas naming the concrete items of Cyrus and children's magazines evokes images in the readers' minds and leads them into the essay in a more interesting manner.

Openings do not need to be wedge-like. Howard Gardner begins a preface more like an umbrella over the whole topic.

> This is a book designed to teach the serious beginning writer the art of fiction.

What a lot we learn from that simple sentence! We can decide immediately whether or not we want to read on. Though this differs from the Sayers opening in many ways, it is similar in that it dives right in.

Gardner's "announcement" style opening is often used. A question opening works also to announce in its own way the upcoming topic. A brief story, called an *anecdote,* is an excellent opening if it fits and leads into the topic. A startling statement or fresh and pertinent quotation can work. Any of these openings must sound honest and appropriate to the theme. They fall flat if they appear to be simply following a formula opening. All those good openings dive right in with no "throat clearing."

Throat clearing is a common habit of writers. They explain how they reached their subject—what they experienced to get there, what people ask in their classes, what they used to think but now see differently—or persuade readers that they need this article. Here is a typical throat clearing from a writer's early draft.

> I felt greatly honored to be invited to be the speaker for the young people at the retreat. I began asking myself what message would encourage them the most. What would challenge them to action? Thinking about possible topics led me to . . .

Openings like that do not often reach print, but when one does we can easily skip it and move on to the message. If we write an opening like that before finally getting to our subject we should ruthlessly delete it, whether it is one sentence or three paragraphs, or more.

Writers often do a better opening after the rest of the essay is finished. By then they can either improve the one they have or write a new one that accurately announces the message that is coming or pulls in the readers with an interesting wedge. After the opening, the middle and end should be united with it as Aristotle wrote.

Let's finish here with two excellent openings. These begin

the first and second chapters of Gardner's book *The Art of Fiction.*

> 1. What the beginning writer ordinarily wants is a set of rules on what to do and what not to do in writing fiction. As we'll see, some general principles can be set down and some very general warnings can be offered; but on the whole the search for aesthetic absolutes is a misapplication of the writer's energy.
> 2. If there are no rules, or none worth his attention, where is the beginning writer to begin?

Point of view. At the beginning of a writing project you need to decide what point of view to use. One choice is to write in first person, using words like *I* and *we.* A ten-year-old's first-person story about his family's Christmas would begin like this.

> My brother and I live with our father and mother. That makes four of us. We love Christmas when we celebrate Christ's birthday. Every year we go to Grandma's house on Christmas Eve.

The boy's real story was written in third person like this.

> Two brothers lived with their father and mother. That made a family of four. They loved Christmas when they celebrate Christ's birthday. Every year they go to their grandma's house on Christmas Eve.

Besides those two points of view, another is second person. That is when you are writing directly *to* someone, as when giving directions for making a craft or finding a house: You go three blocks straight ahead and then turn left.

Fiction writers have many variations of these basic three choices. For instance if they are writing in third person, will

they see events only from the outside or will they see into
people's thoughts? If they can see thoughts, how many characters will they see into? Gardner's book and others on fiction
writing describe these variations in detail. Reading and notic-
ing what authors do is also a good way to learn how to handle
point of view.

This book shifts back and forth mostly between second and
third person because sometimes it is talking to you (you can
try . . .) and sometimes it is talking about other writers (he wrote
about . . .). Occasionally it shifts into first person as I talk about
my thoughts or books. When writing shifts, it should sound natural and fit the message. In fiction, especially, it takes a careful
transition so as not to shock the reader as he finds his view
suddenly shifting without warning.

Abstract and concrete. An important writing principle is to
avoid stating everything in abstract terms as in the preschool
article mentioned earlier. Readers wear out from reading only
high level abstractions, so include illustrations that are concrete
or close to it to help them understand the message. The ladder
below shows gradations of abstractions. The term *liberal arts*
at the top is a highly abstract idea, whereas the doings of the
Main Street bank would provide images closer to concrete.

liberal arts

humanities

sociology

urban living

your town

Main Street

Writers need to use the whole ladder. If an essay stays with
only concrete details near the bottom of a ladder it leaves readers wondering what meaning to make of them. If it stays only
on the higher levels, readers could be frustrated from not understanding well; some specifics would help them. They need for

the writer to constantly move up and down the ladder, giving abstract meanings to concrete details, and the reverse—using concrete details to flesh out abstract meanings.

An example of moving down and then back up the ladder is in my book *World History Made Simple*. To begin telling about Alexander's conquests, it says "Alexander and his army marched through Asia Minor, fighting a Persian army and conquering cities as they went." Fighting and conquering are well up the abstraction ladder. Then the story drops down to details that illustrate the abstractions of fighting and conquering. Priests in Jerusalem risk death by dressing in their priestly robes, meeting Alexander, and surrendering. Alexander outwits the Persian army by silently at night leading part of his army down a steep and dangerous mountain route to surprise the Persians in the morning. After a few paragraphs of such details it moves higher on the ladder again to wrap up the message this way.

> This was only fours years after Alexander first threw his spear into Asian soil. That was lightning speed for an army in those days. They had crossed Asia Minor and pushed into Asia, taking part of Africa, too, along the way.

That was a high-low-high pattern. Many patterns could be used but, by whatever pattern, to hold readers' interest expository writing must have a good mixture of abstract and concrete.

Defining words. Writers do not want to suddenly drop in a big word or technical term that seems to say, "Look what I know!" That's a way to lose readers. It is more courteous to show what the word means. If the word is necessary to the message it is worth taking that space; then the reader does not have to run to a dictionary to figure out what he is reading. (That's a secret to use also when you read; figure out a word from its context and skip the dictionary.)

For the following example, some in the audience may never have heard of *graphic organizer*, but after reading this they have a pretty good idea.

> Graphic organizers accomplish the same effect as outlines but are simpler for some people. These can take any shape that students might invent to help them see what is in the text. They can show a chain of events by connecting them in a line, either vertically or horizontally, or show a family tree to organize who is related to whom. A spider map shows a main item in the center and several lines reaching outward with a label on each. Then horizontal lines with sub-labels can be connected to those. Students who learn a bit about graphic organizers for a reading assignment can later use them even more productively for their writing.

Writing lessons somewhere must teach that writers should start by defining their main words. We see the results in articles in some smaller magazines that begin in dull fashion with a dictionary definition, which is stated in abstract terms. The example above uses concrete illustrations to describe what graphic organizers are. That helps readers more than the dictionary does.

In the next example, the terms *mixed dominance* and *kinesthetic* may be unfamiliar to some readers, but without sounding like a dictionary this teaches what they are.

> Mixed dominance causes reading problems because any sensory message from the right side of the body goes to the left side of the brain and vice versa. Thus if a child is writing with his right hand, that kinesthetic message goes to the left side of his brain. And if his dominant left eye is following the writing, that visual message goes to the right side of the brain. Then the brain has to "stutter" a bit to get the two messages together, and it may settle for seeing the *b* as a *d*.

Often only one sentence will do the job, as in this example.

> Probiotics are supplements of live, friendly bacteria that you can take to enhance or restore a healthy balance in your intestinal tract.

A practical definition like that fits right into the informative article, but the dictionary definition will not fit. It is too high on the abstraction ladder. There it says that *biotics* "refers to life," and the *pro* prefix "advances" something. Readers are better off to learn from the writer.

2. Sentences

This chapter tells what to do after you have written down the message. You need to try being the reader now—a critical reader—to see if it reads smoothly along and if everything is clear. We suggest here some effective techniques for analyzing and improving sentences.

What Is a Sentence?

Definitions. Grammar books think they have to teach you what a sentence is, as though you don't know already. These sections will give you some ideas for talking back to your grammar book in case you want to do that.

Some books say a sentence expresses a complete thought. At least that is simple. Some books are more complex and say that a sentence is a group of words that can stand alone, that are grammatically independent, containing at least one subject and one predicate. Others say it makes a statement, a command, a question, or an exclamation.

H. W. Fowler in his *Dictionary of Modern English Usage* collected ten definitions, and those were only "some examples" he found in grammar books and dictionaries. Fowler did not recommend any of those. Instead, he quoted the definition from the *Oxford English Dictionary* of the mid-1800s, which is a landmark authoritative source of information on Modern English. The *OED* says a sentence is "such portion of a composition or utterance as extends from one full stop to another." In writing, we show full stops by periods, question marks, and exclamation marks. (Fowler should be on the bookshelf of every serious writer. A grammar reference simpler than Fowler's and a good dictionary are necessary, too.)

Grammarians try to come up with a sentence definition that covers all bases and that uses grammatical terms. A college grammar book from my shelf gives one of the typical definitions and then proceeds with nine pages of exceptions—verbless sentences, subjectless sentences, and others. Is that helpful or not? We can't throw out the grammar, but we may want to limit it, especially the grammar that is based on Latin and not on English. An old saying is that if you know the rules well then you know when you can break them.

In the case of sentences, you have been speaking them since you were two or three years old, and reading and writing them since soon after that. Your ear for the language should be pretty good by now if English is your native language. You can evaluate sentences by deciding if they sound right to your ear and if they say clearly what you want to say.

The *OED* definition of a sentence is based not on grammar but on "popular" usage, meaning that it comes from the populace of users of the English language. Many perfectly normal sentences may be only one word or in other ways not meet various grammar requirements. They extend from one "full stop" to the next. Writers often use them to introduce a paragraph, to comment after a sentence, or to answer a question with a simple *no*. Here are some examples from famous authors and from major newspaper editorial pages.

So much for the writings of the first type.

Not that I'm against verbal manipulation.

Tall arrowy white pines.

Once more.

Now for the rest of the story.

Not so fast.

So far, so good.

This type of sentence can also be quite long, as in these examples.

> Better to err a little in the cause of bluntness than to soften the mind with congenital drivel. Better a challenging half-truth than a discredited cliché.

> Not so the maker of verbal blueprints.

The popular definition does not mean that anything goes. Some sentences that you write in a hurry will sound wrong or sick once you examine closer. You probably fix some sentences as you are writing, but then comes a time when you can focus specifically on the sentences. This can become such an interesting job that you may find yourself doing it for all your writing. Famous author James A. Michener said that he could never let something stand as he first wrote it. He revised even his letters, which were meant for an audience of only one. You, too, may find sentences more engrossing than you now think possible.

How To Link Sentences

To begin examining sentences, see if they flow smoothly one after the other. Are thoughts linked together, or must readers think between the sentences to link the thoughts? This principle of linking helps to keep your readers from dropping out. Several techniques for linking sentences follow.

Linking with words. First, we look at techniques for linking with one or two words. The most common conjunctions for linking are *and* and *but.* When you were little maybe you used *and* too often and somebody told you not to begin sentences that way, but there is no rule against it. It is fine to begin with *and* now and then when the meaning requires it. It sounds childish only if you overuse that form.

And signals "straight ahead, keep going." *But* signals "stop, make a sharp turn." If those are the meanings you want, then go ahead and use these good links. You can use them within a sentence to link two clauses together, or you can use them to begin a sentence, thus linking it with the preceding sentence. It is a myth that this is illegal. A major grammar book teaches this:

> It is sometimes claimed that there is a rule against starting a sentence with *and* or *but*, but they are frequently used by experienced writers . . . skilled writers can use these conjunctions with confidence to smooth the flow of the sentence.

If that is not enough for talking back to your grammar book, here is an excerpt from *The New Oxford American Dictionary.*

> It is still widely taught and believed that conjunctions such as *and* [and others] should not be used to start a sentence . . . Writers down the centuries have ignored this advice, however, typically for rhetorical effect . . .

Add *or, yet*, and other conjunctions to that statement.

If you look in any book around your house, especially the Bible, you should find plenty of examples of *and* and *but* at the beginning of sentences, and it is instructive to study those. Do they read smoothly? Do they sound childish? Do you think an editor should have removed any of them? Can you defend what the writer did? (In some books maybe an editor did remove beginning conjunctions.)

Below, are a few other linking words to use. Most are adverbial, and not strictly conjunctions, but they make good links when they convey the exact meaning you need. Do not choose them simply for variety or for decoration. You do not earn a point for using an *ly* word in each paragraph or for using *wherefore*s and *therefore*s. Your reward is in readers who can easily follow what you are trying to say. *However* is not on this list but that troublesome word is discussed separately in the next section.

in addition	certainly	of course
besides	formerly	therefore
yet another	for instance	after
apparently	to illustrate	before
evidently	first (second)	so

Linking with conjunctions has a long history. In 1686, Samuel Johnson wrote an *Address to all English Protestants* and an 1833 reviewer said this about it.

> You cannot alter one conjunction without spoiling the sense. It is a linked strain throughout. In your modern books, for the most part, the sentences in a page have the same connection with each other that marbles have in a bag; they touch without adhering.

Linking with however. Special problems have grown up around the word *however.* Teachers and grammar books started the problems by saying that it is against the law to begin a sentence with *but*, and they want to change it, usually to *however.* If *however* substitutes for *but*, if they are the same in meaning and function, then why are not both of them lawbreakers instead of just one? Why does the computer grammar check catch you up with *but* and let you go scot-free with *however?* Well, somebody who wrote the program believed the myth that *but* should not begin a sentence, and the formula is now in there, at least when your program is set to "formal" and not to "casual."

In spite of the computer programs, *however* does not make a good substitute for *but*. *But* is a conjunction and *however* is an adverb, or call it a conjunctive adverb if you like the grammar jargon. When a writer uses *however*, we should be able to see which action it modifies—something back there in the preceding sentence. But too often it does not modify anything. One grammarian says that amateurs seem to use *however* because they think it looks elegant.

Here is a fictitious example of what could have happened to Mark Twain if he had had a "however" editor. I shortened the sentences for convenience.

> The boys caught fish, cooked supper and ate it, and then fell to guessing at what the village was thinking and saying about them. *However*, when the shadows of night closed them in, they gradually ceased to talk.

The relevant verb in the first sentence is *guessing* (talking), and the *however* adverb means "on the other hand" or "in spite of." Put that together and we read that the boys were talking but on the other hand, or in spite of that, they ceased to talk. Slippery logic. Twain's original *but* signaled a simple turn and did not relate backward as the adverb tries to do.

In all of *Tom Sawyer*, Twain began sentences with *but* 119 times and with *however* only four times. Other good writers follow a similar pattern. The King James Bible contains the word *but* 3994 times and almost half of those begin sentences. *However* occurs zero times.

If someone wants to issue you a ticket for a *but* violation, study your sentences carefully and see if you have grounds for taking the case to court.

Linking with phrases or sentences. Sometimes a phrase instead of a single word makes a more clear meaning than *and*. Does this *and* connection tell enough?

> Archeologists found nine layers of Troy and had to guess which one suffered siege and destruction at the hands of the Greeks. *And* they dated the Trojan War several centuries before Homer.

One possible way to eliminate that vague *and* is to write, *"For several reasons* they dated . . . "* A writer could proceed from there, explaining the reasons or whatever information he plans next. At least we would know that the archeologists did not operate mindlessly. This link makes more sense than just the *and*. (Those archeologists were wrong, though; Homer was not so removed from the war.)

Beyond words and phrases, sometimes a full sentence makes a better link. After a paragraph that details many catastrophic events at the Exodus, the next paragraph begins this way.

> *What an event that was!* Yet historians still wonder. . . .

This first sentence obviously links backward, not just to one preceding sentence but to all the Exodus descriptions. And it allows the writer to smoothly connect the next sentence with *yet*. *Yet* by itself is too weak to connect with the whole paragraph of Exodus catastrophes. The full sentence does the job better.

In an article about sonic booms, this sentence points to what is coming next.

> Here's what you'll need to make your own sonic boom:

After the list of materials and some instructions for making a whip with them, comes a link that points backward to remind readers where they are in the procedure. It works like a signpost along the journey.

> You now have a short whip.

26   *How to Write Clearly*

The writer surely did not need that signpost for himself, but it helps the readers. After plowing through the instructions, they appreciate the chance to pause for a breath. The sign lets them know that they are finished reading the instructions for making the whip, and it implies that the article will now proceed to tell what to do with it, which is exactly what it does. Signs can point to what lies ahead and, as in this example, remind readers of where they have been. They are links along the journey, guiding the reader by connecting thoughts in a meaningful way.

Linking with echoes. Often you can help your readers to continue reading smoothly along by making each sentence pick up an element from near the end of the preceding sentence. In this example the italicized words echo the last word in the preceding sentence. Two of them echo the actual word and one echoes the thought.

> Violent earthshakings always have aftershocks. In this Exodus story, the *aftershocks* lasted many years. For forty *years* the Israelites camped in the desert and met with more upheavals. One time the *earth opened up* and swallowed Korah and his followers who rebelled against Moses and God.

In this next example, the words *son told* echo not the last words, but earlier words in the sentence.

> People in Noah's time held a fresh memory of the great Flood because old man Noah and his sons told them about it. *Son* Shem *told* everybody to fear God and . . .

Compare the following rewrite. All the thoughts are here but they are not related with echoes or any kind of links. That makes it a collection of sentences, not a sequence of sentences, and it results in a choppy read.

> Noah was an old man. The Flood was recent history, and people heard about it. Noah had sons. Shem preached about fearing God. One of Noah's sons was Shem.

Here is an example from Jack London's *The Call of the Wild*. He links mostly by echoing thoughts that carry forward the idea of coming spring. The words change from *spring weather* to *sun rose earlier* to *dawn* to *blaze of sunshine* to *spring murmur,* but the thought of spring echoes from sentence to sentence. The latter sentences contain specific word echoes with *murmur* and *living.* Weather, with different wording, is the subject of every sentence. The gold seekers and their dogs are mentioned just once, and then only because of their relation to the weather; they are not the main subject of the sentence. Here is a master writer linking masterfully.

> It was beautiful spring weather, but neither dogs nor humans were aware of it. Each day the sun rose earlier and set later. It was dawn by three in the morning, and twilight lingered till nine at night. The whole long day was a blaze of sunshine. The ghostly winter silence had given way to the great spring murmur of awakening life. This murmur arose from all the land, fraught with the joy of living. It came from the things that lived and moved again, things which had been as dead and which had not moved during the long months of frost.

Linkage and organization. If you run into too much trouble trying to insert links in a piece of writing, it might be that it needs better organizing. It is not unusual to find at a rewrite stage that the order of things must be juggled around, or some ideas omitted, or another idea inserted. Few writers can fully organize ahead of time, except possibly for short pieces. Linkage and organization are closely related. Organization is the underlying feature, and links make that organization clear to readers, especially in expository writing.

Narrative writing does not need the same kinds of links. In narrative, the events run along in order, and that becomes the linking feature for readers. Extra linking words would detract and appear too wordy.

Together, good organization and linkage provide clarity. Clarity is essential if you want to attract and hold readers, and good linkage is essential to the clarity.

Solving Comma Problems

Commas cause more problems than any other punctuation. A best-selling book by Lynne Truss makes this point by telling about pandas who like to eat the young asparagus-like shoots of the bamboo tree. They eat the leaves too, and practically their whole diet is bamboo. So a writer could say that a panda eats shoots and leaves. Then a "grammar" editor can look at the sentence and see a listing, which for her calls for commas, and add one: "The panda eats, shoots and leaves." The peaceful panda suddenly turned violent, all because of a little comma.

Other examples may not be so humorous, but they can be serious, as well as frustrating to writers who have to fight to retrieve their original meaning. James Thurber is known to have fought with an editor over commas. Mark Twain complained in his humorous style about editors. John Gardner says that punctuation is a subtle art, and its subtlety lies in suspending the rules.

Commas by meaning or by rules? We explore meaning in the next few sections and end with a few grammar rules, as we cannot avoid them entirely.

Commas the easy way. The easiest way to decide troublesome comma problems is by meaning. This is not a new, careless way to use commas, but grammarians and writers have defended it for centuries. The sentences below are the same except for one added comma in the second. This is not funny like the panda sentence; the comma devastates the meaning.

> Animals lived and died, many of them catastrophically
> so they became fossils.
> Animals lived and died, many of them catastrophically,
> so they became fossils.

A creationist wrote this the first way, but a grammarian would want a second comma for one of two reasons—either to precede the conjunction *so* or to complete the parenthetical look of the middle phrase. Reading around the parentheses, then, this says "Animals lived and died . . . so they became fossils." Scientifically that is incorrect. Animals did not become fossils because they died, but because they died catastrophically and thus were buried before their bodies rotted away or were eaten. The first example has the correct meaning; the second looks correct by grammar, but it has the wrong meaning. The little comma makes all the difference.

Commas in the next two examples are not so deadly to the meaning, but they change it slightly or change the emphasis.

> This family activity is so valuable that if you do not
> receive a newspaper yourself, it is worth scrounging some
> up from work or a neighbor or somewhere.

Is it worth scrounging up papers because you don't receive any or because the activity with them is valuable? The comma after the *if* clause leads to the somewhat foolish meaning that you should scrounge up papers if you do not receive any, when the real reason is to do the valuable activity. This sentence reads fine with no comma at all. (By the way, the valuable activity is discussing the political cartoons.)

> This all started back in the days when we had Latin
> grammar schools, and the students actually learned Latin
> and its grammar.

The comma in that example makes it look like a compound sentence with *and* connecting the two parts. But for precise meaning, the last two verbs both belong with *when*—*when* we had schools and *when* the students learned. No comma should separate those.

The meaning approach has no rules for right and wrong. Writers must use common sense, and lean toward helping the reader and not toward satisfying the rigid grammarian.

Commas for smooth reading. If a computer grammar checker is set for "formal," it will recommend commas after the introductory words in the following examples. The computer cannot think like a human can to decide whether or not the reader should pause there. All of these read fine and less pompously with no comma pause.

Somehow, we cannot manage . . .
Thus, we must use . . .
In textbooks, we read . . .
Of course, they always are learning . . .

With somewhat longer introductory phrases writers likewise freely decide whether they want the reader to pause or to read smoothly past the phrase (as in this sentence you are reading). If the wording might cause misreading, then the phrase needs a comma regardless of its length.

Another reason for using fewer commas than grammar rules would allow is that sometimes there are too many and they almost bump into each other.

Pressures today, however, cause people to begin at age five, or earlier, and then . . .

What jerky reading that is! All those commas have grammar

reasons for being there, but not readability reasons. The *however* is there because of the superstition about beginning sentences with *but*. Compare the smooth reading of this alternative.

> But pressures today cause people to begin at age five or earlier, and then . . .

Here is another example with a comma pause about every three words. Try reading it without the first two commas.

> Some children, for various reasons, should start later yet, and some can start earlier.

Commas to avoid misreading. Readers can sometimes misread sentences because of either a missing comma or an extra comma. They may be puzzled and have to reread a sentence to figure out its meaning. Other times they may laugh at the humorous results of a blunder, as with this sentence about Rocky Mountain ticks.

> When not gorged, both male and female are flat, but after feeding the female becomes distended and saclike.

After stumbling a bit, the reader figures out that this means "after feeding, the female becomes distended" and does not mean that somebody was feeding the female. The little comma makes all the difference. If we add a comma after *feeding* we could omit the one after *gorged* to avoid overloading with commas.

The ticks can give people Spotted Fever, and the article further states:

> Although the condition is uncomfortable, other than aspirin or Tylenol, very little can be done to shorten its course.

The two commas enclose what looks like a parenthetical phrase. That enclosing tries to follow a comma rule, but it leaves the meaning ambiguous. Does the sentence mean that we are uncomfortable without aspirin, or that we cannot shorten the fever without aspirin? Removing the first comma would show the most likely meaning. But this still is not a great sentence; the *although* makes a fuzzy relation between clauses.

These next commas were inserted especially to avoid misreading.

> After eating, the cook went back to . . .
> While talking to Marie, Ellen saw . . .
> Protestors threw rocks and bottles, and shots rang out as . . .
> In 1800, 25 people lived in . . .

Commas for emphasis. Writers can emphasize or de-emphasize by judicious use of commas. They also can affect meaning in other subtle ways that defy definition or rules. In this example, a comma affects mostly the emphasis.

> We should delete that throat-clearing opening, whether one sentence or three paragraphs, or more.

The mechanical, rule-based way to handle that sentence would be to treat the three items as a series, all of equal weight: *one sentence, three paragraphs, or more.* An alternative system allows the list with no commas: *one sentence or three paragraphs or more.* That still gives equal weight to all three. The comma, in its subtle way, gives emphasis to *or more.* For still greater emphasis, *or more* could be set off as a separate sentence.

Fowler gives this example where a comma changes the meaning. The first is a matter-of-fact statement and the second indicates indignation by emphasizing the final phrase.

> The master beat the scholar with a strap.
> The master beat the scholar, with a strap.

Sometimes in a series there are commas only, with no *and* before the last item in the list. That punctuation implies that more could be said, that the list is not complete and exact. We see this subtlety of meaning in these next examples.

> Religion, art, politics, manners are either vulgarized or dead or turned into money-making agencies. —Henry Adams
>
> Patrick Henry was then in the youthful vigor of his bounding genius, ardent, acute, eloquent. —Washington Irving

In this next sentence the novelist could have said *the word or the turn of phrase*, but that would imply exactness—these two items and only these two. He used a comma instead of the *or*, and achieved a more subtle meaning that suited his purpose.

> Nature seldom provides me with the word, the turn of phrase, that is appropriate without being farfetched or commonplace.

Commas by grammar. Sometimes we need to pay attention to a bit of grammar and to universal consensus. Everybody agrees on using commas for items in a series, except that they differ over the last item before *and*. A state or country name that follows a city is enclosed with commas before and after it. People often miss that closing comma in sentences because they did not need it on envelopes. A year, as 1776, following a specific date should likewise be enclosed, even though the closing comma is not needed on a letter heading.

Here's a tricky comma problem that often traps writers. In these next examples the middle clause is enclosed with commas in one but not enclosed in the other.

The branch of language *that is called Germanic* is the ancestor of English.

Germanic, *which is the ancestor of English*, differs from the Italic-Latin branch.

In the first example, the middle phrase is essential to the subject; it *defines* what branch we are talking about. We might say it is part of the subject. It takes no commas and usually the word *that*. In the second example, the phrase adds a *comment* on the subject but is not essential to it so it needs commas, and usually the word *which*. Both grammar writers and meaning writers agree on the comma distinction in these meanings, but there is controversy about strictly applying *that* and *which* as explained here. If you can understand the difference between a defining phrase and a commenting phrase you will be ahead of most people in the comma game.

Another universal practice is the way we use commas in dialogue. We place a comma between the quotation and the tag of "he said" or "she answered." When it is not ongoing dialogue but one quotation within a paragraph, writers often omit the comma, particularly when the tag precedes the quotation. They reason that the quotation is the object of a verb: He said "I like it." We do not otherwise put commas between verb and object, and we do not need it here either.

While grammar sometimes helps our comma decisions, it is impossible to decide by logic of grammar alone. We achieve better readability by using the meaning approach first and then a bit of grammar when we need it. Some books use the terms *close* and *open* to refer to the two ways of handling commas. Grammar books that teach the close system may say to *always* observe this or that rule. Some people like to cross out that *always*. Writers with the open approach follow the principle of using only as many comma pauses as will help the reader, and not more.

Doctoring Sentences

Active and passive. The subject in sentences usually acts. We call that *active voice.* In other sentences the subject is acted upon and we call that *passive voice.* Writers try not to use too many passive sentences because active voice enlivens their stories. Here are examples of passive sentences contrasted with their active form.

> The pyramids *are guarded* by a huge sculpture called a Sphinx.
> Active: A huge sculpture called a Sphinx *guards* the pyramids.
>
> This course will *be taught by* CPR professionals.
> Active: CPR professionals will *teach* this course.

Sometimes a writer seems to work at avoiding active voice. Here, two obvious active forms jump to mind, but the original writer used neither.

> Thirteen students *have been awarded* scholarships from . . .
> Active: Thirteen students *received* scholarships from . . .
> Active: The company *awarded* scholarships to thirteen . . .

Those read better in the active voice, but there are times when the best choice is passive. Here is one. In an old Greek myth, Persephone had to be in the underground for much of the year but each spring she could come back. One writer tells it this way.

> Her mother grieved, nothing grew, and there was winter on the earth. But as soon as Persephone's footsteps *were heard*, the whole earth burst into bloom. Spring had come.

To change *were heard* into active, the author would need a subject to do the hearing. He probably didn't want to say that just the mother heard. He could have said "all the people" heard, but that suddenly brings in a new subject that hasn't been in the story. It also raises an image of loud, thundering steps heard throughout the land. This passive version allows the romantic image that the bursting of spring everywhere is the footfall of Persephone. The poet Sappho used that image, and wrote "I heard the footfall of the flower spring." The author's use of passive in the Persephone story seems to be an excellent choice. It is difficult to think of a better wording.

A third kind of sentence to add to active and passive is the linking sentence. This grammar term is not the same as the linking techniques discussed earlier. This joins two sentence parts together with some form of *to be* or with a few other verbs like *seem, feel,* or *sounds.* Experienced writers try not to use linking sentences when the thought really is active. To do so results in noun writing. Here is a linking sentence and two possible ways to recast it to avoid noun writing.

> Linking sentence: The tendency [noun] is to seek answers from...
>
> Active: We tend [verb] to seek...
>
> Active: People tend to seek...

Most writing teachers advocate using active sentences as often as possible, to achieve more vigorous writing. The other side reminds us that passive can sound more literary and in some cases can fit the purpose better, as in the Persephone example. The best procedure is to avoid sliding carelessly into passive; use it only when it is the best choice.

Rhythm and sound. Rhythm is an important aspect of English prose writing style. No poetry book rules or any kind of rules can guide in this elusive feature of language. We do not want to overdo it and sound like JACK and JILL went UP the HILL. In fact, if a sentence accidentally falls into such a pattern we would change the wording to avoid it. Neither do we want the rhythm of a more sophisticated poem; we're writing prose after all.

But even for prose, a good way to develop our ear for rhythm and sound is to study poems and try to write some. Lesson books often say to write something short like haiku because lessons like to aim for producing a finished product. Here, though, we are more interested in the process—the hearing and experimenting with language sounds. Reading and trying to imitate favorite poems is a good way to do this.

English with its short words is more graceful than highly inflected languages with suffixes and prefixes attached to many words. In the lines below, more than half the words are only one syllable. Besides the end rhymes, there are interior vowel rhymes of m*e* with d*ee*pens and m*e* with *e*ventide, and other vowel effects in these lines. Also, there is consonant alliteration of *f*ast *f*alls and of *d*arkness *d*eepens. Henry Lyte may not have thought of all those phonics details, but he certainly chose words that sounded best.

> Abide with me, fast falls the eventide;
> The darkness deepens; Lord, with me abide.

Much is lost if we change only a few words while retaining the rhythm pattern and the end rhyme.

> Abide with me; encroaching eventide
> Brings gloomy darkness; Lord, with me abide.

In prose, writers naturally do not want strong poetry rhythm. But good prose has subtle rhythm anyway. The rhythm feature is most noticeable when it is not there, when the writing sounds clumsy. During revisions, writers may lengthen or shorten sentences and juggle words in various ways. A lot of that is to make the meaning clearer, but some is to make it sound better. Writing lessons usually remind beginners to vary their sentence lengths, and when they change a sentence simply for variety of length they may overload it or lose its focus. The cure can be worse than the disease, but the principle remains that sentences should not be too much alike. Short sentences move the thoughts along briskly; longer sentences are more reflective. Too much repetition of either kind becomes boring, especially if they are similar in construction. Sentence length is just one aspect of the larger principle of rhythm.

Writers work on rhythm and sound, sometimes not able to analyze why they like it better a certain way, but their ear tells them it is better. Here is a line of prose with several rewritings, all understandable, but lacking the rhythmic touch of a talented writer.

> Trees were sparsely spread over the land, their branches stripped of leaves, and the air was cold.
>
> The few trees in sight had already lost their summer leaves, and the weather was cold.
>
> There were only a few barren trees, and it was cold.

Here is the original line as C. S. Lewis wrote it.

> There were few trees and bare, and it was cold.

Professors see that people with the best ear for rhythm are those most steeped in the writings of skilled masters past and present, writers not only of great literature but also of good expository prose.

Sick sentences. After fixing commas and links and other matters mentioned earlier, some undiagnosed sentences remain sick. Many of these—probably most—can be cured best by attending to the meaning. Here's a little contest between a computer, which is rule-based, and a human, who is a thinking creature. The human put in a sentence copied from a magazine.

Human:	Though only seven years old, his son and he drifted apart.
Computer:	Fragment (no suggestions)
Human:	OK, I'll add subject and verb to the opening. Though *he was* only seven years old, his son and he drifted apart.
Computer:	
Human:	That's crazy. It should object to that senseless sentence. I'll try the original opening with a sensible ending. Though only seven years old, he could read fifth grade books.
Computer:	However,
Human:	Well, I'll press "change" and try that.
Computer:	However, only seven years old, he could read fifth grade books.
Human:	I give up; my computer's not very smart.

True. A human brain does better with sentence meanings. On that original sentence the computer did not care at all which person was seven years old. Here is a sentence that passes the computer without the blink of an eye at the sight of Don's family homeschooling at conventions.

> Don, popular author and speaker, shares his twenty years experience homeschooling his nine children at conventions across the country.

That is not deadly; readers can catch the meaning. But it would better be made into two sentences or at least recast in some way. Here is one possibility.

> Don, popular author and speaker, who has homeschooled nine children for twenty years, shares that experience at conventions across the country.

The computer would not blink at this next sentence either. Both clauses are complete with subject and verb, and a comma and connector *although* are in place. It looks entirely proper grammatically.

> We did not enjoy the comedian's jokes, although he was first on the program.

That is wrong by meaning, not by grammar. No relating word can replace *although*, because the two clauses simply are not related. That sentence cannot be fixed. The only remedy is to say something different. This meaning could work.

> Other people laughed at the comedian's jokes, but we did not enjoy them.

Here is another sentence that cannot be fixed, because the

two parts do not relate with its *but* or with any connecting word. The meaning must be changed.

> Writing can be revised endlessly, but the first step towards communicating your thoughts is to feel able to put them down on paper.
>
> Possible revision: You can revise later, but the first step is to . . .

Vague words commonly make sentences sick. We can easily read every word of this next sentence but *movement*, *skills*, and *abilities* are abstract. Each can include so many things that the sentence becomes a highly generalized statement. Generalizations have their place, but in this context of teaching children to memorize it is weak.

> Pairing movement with memory skills will increase a child's memorization abilities.

Since the writer did not clearly tell us what to do, we have to figure out our own teaching system. Here's one.

> Letting the active child jump or clap while he recites his times tables will help him memorize them.

What are memory *skills* and *abilities?* Can the writer name even one, or is that just jargon to make the sentence sound properly educational? Teachers can pair movement (of some kind) with memory *practice* (on something), but how would they combine it with *skill?* Vague words signal vague thinking. Either the writer works hard to write clearly, or the reader must work hard to extract some measure of meaning.

Parallelism. This is not geometry; we're still talking about writing. For an example of what parallel construction does for

sentences, let's begin by looking at this sentence that carries a
serious message.

> We need to keep this system of government in which
> citizens have the power to govern themselves and choose
> what is best for them.

Important thoughts are there but in a mundane and forgettable
sentence. Here now is the unforgettable version.

> We resolve . . . that the government of the people, by the
> people, and for the people shall not perish from the earth.

Here, again, are some unforgettable words, this time from
Winston Churchill speaking to Parliament.

> We shall go on to the end, we shall fight in France, we
> shall fight on the seas and oceans, we shall fight with
> growing confidence and growing strength in the air, we
> shall defend our Island whatever the cost may be, we shall
> fight on the beaches, we shall fight on the landing grounds,
> we shall fight in the fields and in the streets, we shall fight
> in the hills; we shall never surrender . . .

That is the almost lost art of grand oratory. On paper we
cannot thunder like that, but we can enjoy reading these, without
an amateur sing-song rhythm, but with the power of a higher
rhythm carried along by parallel construction.

Though our everyday sentences will not live for centuries,
many of them at least will read more smoothly and clearly if we
recast them into parallel form. Here are some examples.

> In short order, the flood was followed by torrential rains
> and then later two snowstorms came.
>
>   . . . followed by torrential rains and then by two snow-
> storms.

Children should learn to be good stewards of resources and how money works.

. . . learn how money works and how to be good stewards of it.

. . . learn how money works and how to use it well.

He traveled throughout the Rocky Mountains and carrying the gospel wherever he went.

. . . traveled throughout . . . and carried the gospel . . .

This curriculum is easy to understand and the preparation is simple.

. . . easy to understand and simple to prepare.

Sometimes we may prefer that writers not cure their sentences. Life is more interesting with sentences like these.

They took the road out of the city.

We had a dog show up at our place today.

A car was in the middle of the river which had obviously been washed off the road at the height of the flood.

An ad: First, she was taken with fruits and vegetables. Next, she was inspired by popcorn, footballs and sharks. Then one day Nicole Miller was struck by a Mercedes-Benz.

3. Words

Writers choose words while first writing the message and later as they change and move words during revision. Throughout the process, words play a basic role. In this chapter we focus on some of the word work that careful writers do.

Choosing Words

Denotation or connotation. The dictionary definition of a word is an explicit meaning (or meanings) that we call *denotation.* But out in the real world, in the context settings, words can suggest moods or meanings not specified in the dictionary. We call those meanings their *connotations.*

Skillful writers, by understanding these two kinds of meanings, can choose their wording according to the moods or opinions they want to build in their readers. One reporter can write that the price of something *surged* up, while another writes that it *edged* upward, both reporters using the same price figures. Others could say the price *jumped* or *climbed* or *rose.* The words all denote the same thing—a price rise—but they connote various attitudes the writers wish to convey.

Propagandists make good use of word connotations. Groups today with political agendas use clever word choices in even their names. The Association of American Trial Lawyers became known for bringing frivolous lawsuits against corporations or anybody who had plenty of money, and that brought the term "trial lawyers" into disrepute among the general public. So the association changed its name to American Association for Justice. America—justice—those certainly connote virtues. The American Civil Liberties Union also has a name that wraps itself in the flag. But its founder, in his own words, was "for socialism, disarmament and ultimately the abolishing of the state itself." Those still are aims of the Union. Their name does not explicitly describe who they are, but rather it connotes what they want people to think they are. Perceptive readers learn to see through the wording of propagandists.

Writers who think, even though not propagandists, need to understand the two kinds of meanings—denotation and connotation. Word denotations come from dictionary definitions. Word connotations come from the real world of reading and using the language.

Tone. Choosing words for their connotation affects the tone. Here is a classroom story about tone.

A teacher passed out a copy of a news story to her class and instructed them to read it silently and decide whether they were on the side of the county officials or of the citizens. The class did not know it, but each side of the room received a different version of the story. Both versions gave the same information, but they were worded differently. Below, we see the opening sentences of the two versions.

> Came the knock on the door, the flash of authority, the midnight ride to headquarters—and 14 persons faced the desk sergeant on charges of failing to return overdue library books. "They slammed us in a cell, allowed us one phone call and told us bail was $200," said Robert Ansley, 36, a salesman.

> Washington County library, after months of sending overdue notices and certified letters, finally resorted to having 14 people arrested for failing to return books. "These people defied authority," said Magistrate Avery Wilkins. "That is why we charged them."

It is easy to guess how each side of the class voted. The knock on the door and the midnight ride are reminiscent of Hitler rounding up Jews. The flash of authority could be simply a policeman identifying himself at the door. Facing the desk sergeant sounds like a confrontation instead of a routine registration of an arrested person. And the word *slammed* connotes a hostility that would not be implied if this reported simply that the people were jailed. (Curious? The first example was the original as it appeared in the newspaper, and the second was the teacher's rewrite.)

Writers choose not only what details to report but also what words to use in order to promote the mood they want in their readers. Below are descriptions of mountains and sun from two stories. We see the first description through the eyes of Jack London's avaricious gold rushers and the second through the eyes of happy children in my book *The Cabin and the Ice Palace*. Words like *naked*, *eternal*, and *dancing* affect the mood, turning it to a tone of harshness or of beauty.

> They shivered under the midnight sun on the naked mountains between the timberline and the eternal snows, and dropped into summer valleys amid swarming gnats and flies.
>
> The mountains stood grand and dignified, sunlight dancing about them. Wind chased their snow off into the blue sky.

Various tones that writers can show include humor, seriousness, lightness, irony, excitement—whatever is appropriate to the subject. Some tones to avoid in serious writing are exaggeration and dogmatism, though these could be used for humor or irony. Inexperienced writers sometimes try to convey tone by punctuation—scattering exclamation marks to show excitement, or putting question marks within parentheses to show irony. These need rewriting; the words, not the graphics, should convey the meaning.

Metaphor pictures. Most people use metaphors almost without thinking, to say the engine died, we had a blast, or she's a doll. One writer said there is a teaspoon of truth to the claim. Another said that workbooks have no afterlife. The word pictures are metaphors. Mark Twain, a self-taught writer, was a master of word pictures. In the passage below we need to know that Twain was touring Europe and he had earlier told about gas lanterns along the railway beside the city of Heidelberg (before electricity).

> One thinks Heidelberg by day—with its surroundings— is the last possibility of the beautiful; but when he sees Heidelberg at night, *a fallen Milky Way*, with that glittering railway *constellation* pinned to the border, he requires time to consider upon the verdict.

Twain used the mass of sparkling Milky Way stars as a metaphor to stand for the view of the night city. Then he called the line of railway lights a *constellation*, and that carried on the same metaphor. With that picture, he figured that people should change their minds about daytime Heidelberg being so beautiful that nothing could surpass it.

To understand one of the metaphors below about the ruined castle we need to know that in Twain's day Edward Lear (yes, the limerick writer) was a beloved artist who painted landscapes and birds—that is, living things. But the castle is not living; it is inanimate. Twain called it a Lear painting anyway, and that characterized it as more living and beautiful than if he had described old ruined stone walls. Two more word pictures are also marked with italics.

Out of the billowy upheaval of vivid green foliage, *a rifle-shot removed*, rises the huge ruin of Heidelberg Castle, with empty window arches, *ivy-mailed battlements*, moldering towers—*the Lear of inanimate nature*—deserted, discrowned, beaten by the storms, but royal still, and beautiful.

A rifle shot removed tells approximate distance to anyone familiar with rifles. *Ivy-mailed battlements* cleverly makes ivy on the walls to be like the flexible metal armor that ancient soldiers wore. That defensive war image goes along with calling the castle walls its battlements; the walls and the armor are both defensive. Twain probably coined the word *discrowned*, but we have no trouble seeing how it applies to the castle that once protected reigning kings but then lay in ruins.

In our day we have TV, movies, and easy travel, and we learn what buildings and rivers are like in other parts of the world, so writers do not describe in such detail as Twain. But metaphors have not gone out of style. A metaphorical image of just a couple of words can take the place of many words, and some writers say they use metaphors for that reason—to save words. How many words would a writer need to explain what he means by *teeth* in the law or *eye* of the storm?

Verb pictures. Adjectives and metaphors are not the only ways to paint word pictures. Twain used verbs also, as we see in the paragraph below. He was at the upper end of the gorge watching the river rushing through and described it with many verbs. Twain used adjectives, too, but let's pass those by for now while we observe how he used verbs (and related words). The sentences are longer than is the style today, but we can learn from them anyway, reading slowly through the long sentences.

This gorge—along whose bottom *pours* the swift Neckar—is *confined* between a couple of long, steep ridges, a thousand feet high and densely *wooded* clear to their summits, with the exception of one section which has been *shaved* and *put* under cultivation. These ridges are *chopped off* at the mouth of the gorge and *form* two bold and conspicuous headlands, with Heidelberg *nestling* between them; from their bases *spreads away* the vast dim expanse of the Rhine valley, and into this expanse the Neckar *goes wandering* in shining curves and *is* soon *lost* to view.

Adjective pictures. In that last example, Twain seemed not to be thinking "Oh, this is a description now, so I need some adjectives for the landscape." Nobody writes by grammar like that. Experienced writers think of what they want to say instead of thinking about grammar. They think of developing images and moods and of telling information clearly. When young students are told to use adjectives, they may write sing-songy like this:

We saw a small, white house with a neat, green lawn.

An older student trying to use adjectives wrote like this.

The *blue-green* waves from the lake can be heard as you approach the *rustic* cabin. In the midst of a *fragrant* pine forest the *contented* cabin rests, keeping a *watchful* eye on the *turbulent* lake . . . the *lonely* cabin presents a *quiet, peaceful* scene to the *unwary* traveler . . .

Is there danger, or not? These contrived adjectives are not harmonious. The lake at first had presumably beautiful blue-green waves (when you could hear but not yet see them) and then later the waves are said to be turbulent. The cabin is contented, but keeps out a watchful eye, and travelers must be wary—of something. But there are a lot of interesting adjectives. Did the student earn a point for each one?

Another student made a sudden change in this example that uses verbs as well as adjectives.

> I climbed up the cold, gray steps, opened the stiff, squeaky door, slipped through the narrow, dark hall, and at last fell comfortably into my deep, soft chair.

That is a fine sample of using adjectives, according to a "grammar" book. But a "meaning" book like this disagrees. Something is wrong if the reader is all set for a scary encounter and suddenly is plumped down into a comfortable easy chair. Writers must think of the readers and of the moods and images they build for them, whether they use verbs or adjectives or noun metaphors.

Today's style is to go easy on adjectives. We should use them judiciously when we need them, but they are not ordinarily the route to good descriptions.

Moving and Changing Words

Wandering words. Only and *either* are two words that commonly wander from their best home. Other words can wander too.

> I am *only* a mom of two.
> I am a mom of *only* two.
>
> *Either* send a letter or an e-mail.
> Send *either* a letter or an e-mail.
>
> He was *even* angry at the legislature's action.
> He was angry *even* at the legislature's action.

Misplaced modifiers change the meaning. Does this sentence tell what children *learn* better or what they *remember* better?

> Children will remember what they have learned *better* if they practice it.
> Children will remember *better* what they have learned if they practice it.

These next examples need various kinds of surgery because of words and phrases that are out of place.

> Our college is serving young people desiring a quality liberal arts education for over 150 years. (Are they recruiting ancient students?)
> Garth Linton was sentenced to 12 years in prison for attempted robbery with a gun last week. (Does the sheriff's department close every case so quickly?)
> One of my goals is to fix up this antique house for the next 100 years. (Does he expect such a long life?)

Hidden verbs. Writing sounds dull when verb ideas are hidden in some other words. Using the real verb perks up the reading noticeably.

> Both approaches should be useful in *assisting* children in *memorization.*
> Both approaches should *help* children *to memorize.*
> He gave *suggested* uses for . . .
> He *suggested* uses for . . .
> We are already in *agreement.*
> We already *agree.*
> One of the easiest ways to raise funds for the school is *the purchase of* grocery certificates.

In the last sentence we could change the noun phrase to *to purchase*, but that still does not pass strict inspection. Do the fund raisers purchase the certificates or are parents to purchase them? When parents purchase, are they raising funds or giving donations? This sentence is not fatal since we know what the writer wants to say, but she could change the colorless *one . . . is* subject and verb to the more active *you can help*, and clarify part of her meaning this way.

> You can help us raise funds by purchasing grocery certificates.

Science writers are more prone to this noun writing than we normal people.

> Ongoing tentativeness becomes implementable when recursion is the major research process used.
>
> Attempted translation: We can hold only tentative conclusions if we constantly add more data.

Most writing teachers advocate using a verb style of writing rather than a noun style, but some say let's not carry that too far; a noun style is not necessarily "bad." It sounds more literary and it has its place.

> Human courage should rise to the height of human calamity.—Robert E. Lee
>
> Of making many books there is no end; and much study is a weariness of the flesh.—Solomon

Excess words. Sometimes small words in a sentence perform no useful function, and are better omitted.

> Ivan *was a boy who* liked to read historical novels.
> Ivan liked to read historical novels.
>
> Writing *was something that* Frank didn't like.
> Frank didn't like writing.
>
> Textbooks try to cover all *of the* important topics.
> Textbooks try to cover all important topics.

One excess *of the* probably will not bother readers, but if these are repeated throughout a paragraph or essay they become irritating. The word *the* deserves separate mention. As a definite article it refers to something specific, in this case a specific group of topics. If this group had been mentioned or defined previously, then a better linking word would be *those.* But if this means important topics in general, then *the* can be omitted. People don't usually think of omitting *the*, but try it for a while and see how you like the effect.

You can often omit *there* and *it* at the beginning of sentences and use a better subject instead.

> *There* are not many topics more important than . . .
> Not many topics are more important than . . .

Better yet, avoid the negative and begin: An important topic is . . .

Some phrases like *in terms of* and *related to* seem to be used more by adults than by students. Here are a few examples.

> Those children do well *in terms of* academic achievement.
> Those children do well academically.
>
> We read several books *related to* Greek history.
> We read several books about Greek history.

A second *factor for* why . . .
A second reason why . . . (A second reason is . . .)

. . . distractions that *are attendant to* a peer group.
. . . distractions of a peer group.

Intensifiers like *very, such, too, highly,* and *extremely* work with spoken language because the stress and tone of voice give the desired emphasis. But in writing, these words usually seem weak. How heavy is *very* heavy? How good is *such* a good time? One grammarian says that *so* as an intensifier sounds schoolgirlish: The book was *so* long. Better to say it was *so* long that we couldn't finish it in one night. Or say simply that it is a long book.

We need no intensifier before a word that is absolute. If something is unique, then *very* unique or *extremely* unique add nothing to the meaning. If something is obvious, it helps not at all to say it is *abundantly* obvious; if essential, it is already *absolutely* essential. To use or not use the extra words mentioned earlier is a choice for writers to judge. But this warning about absolute words is close to a law, except for dialogue where the writing imitates speech.

We can omit final verbs in sentences or clauses like the next examples. Grammar zealots say we need them, but many good writers prefer to omit them.

The children who began to study phonics earlier did not learn more than the others *did.*
Not all children are as bright as Johnny *is,* but . . .

Some grammar books say to add *that* in sentences like these next. But in the paragraphs above, *that* is omitted. Did you stumble over the meanings of these sentences when a *that* was omitted?

> Grammar zealots say *that* we need them.
> Better to say *that* it was so long that . . .

Add words or omit words? Writers with their ear for English make their own decisions.

Redundant words. When removing excess words we need to stop at some reasonable point. English language is so redundant that we nearly always see a word that could be removed. The sentences below are progressively shortened, but the final two-word version contains the whole command included in the top nine-word version.

> Read all of this clear through to the end.
> Read this clear through to the end.
> Read this through to the end.
> Read this clear to the end.
> Read all of this.
> Read this all.
> Read this.

A writer must choose according to context, tone, courtesy, and other commonsense considerations. My context for this sentence was to tell friends how to read a humorous story that I sent them. They had to read it thoroughly without skipping any parts in order to appreciate the laugh-out-loud ending. So I wrote: Read this clear through to the end. Lots of redundancy there, but they laughed out loud.

Accidental words. Some words show up simply by accident. Here are examples.

> There was *one* mountain lion sighting *one* night in Crescent Park.

> The hardware store *can* order a bear resistant trash *can* for you.
>
> As she grew older, her face acquired a beauty that sur*passed* that of her *past*.
>
> That paragraph has a *consistent* topic string *consisting* of physicians and diagnoses.

That fourth accident happened to a writing teacher, no less. These examples are a special case where the same word has two uses or two meanings. These are not to say that you should go to the thesaurus and find synonyms so as not to repeat words. For clarity, you often *should* repeat words exactly. But repair the injured sentences.

Long words. *Use* is a perfectly good word that can be either a noun or verb, but awhile back it became fashionable to say *utilize.* That naturally needed the forms *utilized* and *utilizing.* Next, if one needed a noun form it became *utilization.* What's next? Utilizationally? Actually, both *use* and *utilize* are legitimate words, of Old French origin, but the meanings are slightly different. *Utilize,* in appropriate contexts, means to make practical and efficient use of something. A nutrition article says that flavonoids from fruits and vegetables enhance the effects of vitamin C, thus helping the body to utilize vitamin C more fully. *Utilize* is more formal and should be used sparingly lest the writing strike readers as pretentious. Some writers seem to utilize everything while most of us simply use them. The King James Bible never uses the word *utilize.*

The same story fits the word *methodology.* It has become jargon for the simple words *method* or *methods.* The suffix *ology* means "the study of" something. So a college education course may take up the study of methods and list methodology as its topic, but individual teachers do not use or prefer this or that methodology. A curriculum does not use a methodology. A writer or speaker cannot recommend a methodology. All these uses require the plain word *method.*

Fiction characters may *survey the area* instead of looking around. Or they may *calculate* instead of think. A newspaper reported that a rocket *achieved orbital insertion* instead of went into orbit. If we sense that a writer aims mainly for elegant verbal effect, that mannerism distracts us. Plain English does not distract readers.

Pesky pronouns. Pronouns get misused more than other words because so much grammar affects them. They change into more forms than other words. They change for subject and object (I, me), for person (I, you, he and she), and for gender (he, she, it). They also change for singular and plural, as do the nouns and verbs. This is not a grammar book, and we cannot cover the grammar of pronouns but will point out just some areas that most affect writing.

1. First, it must be clear in every case what each pronoun stands for. A writer has someone in mind when he writes *he* or *they.* But for the reader to call the same persons to mind, the pronoun must link back clearly to the intended persons. Sometimes there are two boys in the preceding sentence and a *he* could refer to either of them. Sometimes too many sentences come between the boy's name and the *he.* To fix it, the writer can name the boy again or in other ways change the wording to make the meaning clear. The principle to know is that every pronoun must have a clear antecedent.

2. Another principle is that pronouns should agree in number, that is singular with singular and plural with plural. Ordinarily we find that easy. We say Rick sharpened *his* knife or the boys sharpened *their* knives. But the "political correctness"

crowd has manufactured a problem in recent times by trying to change a long-time historic meaning of *his*. For good reasons people have used *his* in a generic manner to refer to a child or student or citizen or any person of unspecified sex. Recently though, people in the feminist movement complain that it is unfair to women and girls to say *his*. They don't want us to write that the student forgot *his* book, but we should say *his or her* book. Or to avoid that clumsiness they use plural pronouns, and it is common now to see sentences like these in print.

> Each child works at *their* own level.
> When a child learns this way, *they* can remember better what *they* have learned.
> A person can develop in math even though *their* main talent is in language.

Writers can sometimes avoid the problem by changing the subject to plural. Those three sentences all could begin with plural subjects, but that will not work everywhere. So we have a choice of using *his* (and *he*) in the historical manner or of capitulating to the complainers.

I choose not to capitulate; writing is more graceful the old way. If enough of us fight the change we can keep the dictionaries on our side. Homeschoolers showed in the 1980s that they can influence dictionaries. At the beginning of the decade, high level publications printed *home school* in two words like high school. But homeschoolers, logically, realized that they had a unique entity called a homeschool. Also they needed an adjective, as well as a verb along with its *ed* and *ing* endings. Enough homeschoolers wrote so sensibly that by the end of the decade *homeschool* and its derivatives appeared officially in dictionaries, and the New York Times and other publications began to use it.

The same story goes for the word *man*, one dictionary definition of which is "the human race; humankind." Another definition says it refers to Homo sapiens either collectively or individually without regard to sex. This important word began with God at the creation of man, and in English it has been used universally in literature and non-fiction. If we capitulate, mankind will lose a lot and gain nothing.

So will we ungrammatically mix plural pronouns with singular subjects and help that to become Standard English? Will we drop most uses of *man*? Or will we help to save real English from degeneration?

3. We do not need grammar lessons to learn to say *I* hiked or *I* bought something. We never miss that pronoun when it is the subject. We also have no trouble using the object form—to *me*, for *me*, showed *me*. That is, when the pronoun is the object of a preposition or verb, we naturally say *me*. But a problem erupts when another person enters the phrase: for Jenny and me, showed Gene and me. Surprisingly often, speakers and writers use *I* in such phrases. We can hear that any day in radio sermons and talk shows. This is wrong by both the rule system and the natural English system of word order. The easiest way to get this right is to omit momentarily the name Jenny and see if we would say *for I* or *for me*. How simple! How did our high school English manage to make such a complex problem out of this? All the same reasoning applies to deciding between *he* and *him* and between *she* and *her.*

My guess about the source of this error is the high school grammar teaching that the verb *to be* in all its forms does not take objects. Instead, it links the subject with another name for the same subject: *It* is a *ball*; The *actor* is *Jim*. The following diagrams compare a linking sentence with an active sentence.

Active sentence: subject → transitive verb → object
Linking sentence:
        subject → linking verb → subject complement

In the linking sentence both substantives refer to the subject of the sentence. Thus we should say *It is I*, according to grammar. That gets so pounded into high schoolers' heads that they learn half the rule anyway. They learn that it is more elegant and correct to say *I* at the end of a sentence and they fail to learn to do that only in a linking sentence. This leads to the strange twist that educated people make the mistake more often than the less educated who end sentences with *me*, as is natural in English. The I-me problems appear not only in speech but also in print where people supposedly have more time to think and correct a misuse. Here is a newspaper quote from a cat in an animal shelter.

> The adoption fee for my brother and *I* is $75 each and it covers most shots.

That sentence is wrong by both systems. English word-order wants *me* at the end of the phrase, and rule-based grammar wants *me* as the object of the preposition *for.* It's only the half-learned high school teaching that could put *I* in this sentence.

Some grammar books have caught on to the conflict of the two systems and acknowledge now that in linking sentences it can be OK to use the objective pronoun. That is, we can say "It's me," except in the most formal writing.

4. The who-whom problem is related in that it helps—most of the time—to know that *who* is subjective and *whom* is objective. For the complexities of who and whom, we can refer to grammarians. Fowler has several pages of fine print on this. For checking on small pronoun matters, like singular or plural, dictionaries are often the best resource.

Infinitives. It is a myth that we should not split infinitives— verb forms *to eat*, *to run*, and so on. We inherit that myth because Latin infinitives are one word and cannot be divided, so the myth says we should not divide them in English either.

Dictionaries that define *split infinitive* call it an arbitrary rule, an unreasonable rule, or a so-called rule. Having this myth in our books causes many writing mistakes and awkwardisms. Our natural ear for English would not split infinitives often, but occasionally we need to split one to make the meaning clear. In this example, avoiding the split infinitive attaches the adverb *powerfully* to the wrong verb. It says it *tends* powerfully instead of *moves* powerfully.

> That writing tends powerfully *to move* the heart.
> That writing tends *to* powerfully *move* the heart.

In some cases we can avoid splitting by moving the adverb, but we may like the split version better.

> I was able *to* correctly *identify* every one.
> I was able *to identify* correctly every one.
> I was able correctly *to identify* every one.

The word *not* improves many infinitives by splitting them, as in this example. We can see how awkward it would sound to place the *not* either before or after this infinitive.

> We have *to* not *panic.*

Grammarian Fowler divided people into five classes depending on their attitude toward split infinitives. The classes range from those who neither know nor care what a split infinitive is to those who know and can distinguish the best choice to make in each sentence. In between are people who avoid split infinitives even at the cost of committing a worse sin than the "tending powerfully" example given above. Those in-between writers would have great difficulty trying to unsplit this:

> He was obliged *to* more than *double* the price.

Correct usage. Principles and preferences and ear for language govern most of the word usages discussed so far. But some matters are governed by consensus of English users and are set down in dictionaries. The list below gives a few words that are often misused, even finding their way into print. Choices between one word or two come first on the list. The rest are alphabetical.

A lot is always two words, never one.

All right does not follow the pattern of *already* and *altogether.* Its proper form is two words. One of its meanings is OK, as in "All right, I'll go with you." Another meaning is safe and sound, as in "Are you all right?" Dictionaries show still more meanings. You will sometimes see *alright* in print, but don't add to them.

A while is two words when a preceding preposition needs *while* for an object, as in "for a while" and "after a while." Less commonly this is an adverb and remains one word, as in "wait awhile" and "work awhile." A few decades ago a grammarian said that the one-word use may become standard for both meanings. So far his prediction has not come true.

Every day is joined together only for adjective use, as in *everyday* clothes. Otherwise it is two words, as in *every day* the weather grows colder or she studies *every day.*

High school is two words for all uses in most stylebooks, though some allow one word for adjective use. *Homeschool* has now become one word for noun, adjective, and even for verb use.

Into, onto and other doubled prepositions sometimes are two words instead of one. Could we drive down the street and turn *into* McDonalds? Or is it better to turn *in* to McDonalds?

Do students turn a paper *into* their teacher, or turn it *in* to her? The *in* in these cases is an adverb telling where. When a computer suggests changing one of these, it really is just asking us to think and decide. The computer can't decide.

Effect is usually a noun and *affect* a verb, as in the examples below. Reference books show some additional, rare uses besides these.

> Dr. Howard explained what a black hole is and described its *effects* [noun] on surrounding objects. The curvature of space *affects* [verb] the motion of objects in space.

Farther and *further* are not quite synonyms. *Farther* refers to actual physical distance, as to run *farther* today than yesterday. *Further* means more. We might say that it refers to figurative distance, as with *further* thought or *further* study he changed his mind.

Use *fewer* for items we can count: fewer trees, fewer calories, fewer hours. Use *less* for uncountable quantities: less shade, less food, less time.

Led is the past tense of *lead*. This does not follow the pattern of *read*, where past and present tense are both spelled *read*. We do that, presumably, to avoid writing that we *red* the book last night. *Read* is thus called an irregular verb, because it does not form past tense in the regular way. Other verbs, like *lead*, *feed*, and *breed*, are regular verbs and they do change spelling for past tense.

Lose and *loose* are different words that do not sound alike or spell alike, or mean the same.

Peaked and *piqued* are different words with different meanings, though pronounced alike.

Careful writers find they use dictionaries and grammar reference books more for such small, common words than for looking up big, unfamiliar words. A writer using a word like *pharmacology* is not likely to misuse it, but in the same article he may misuse *awhile* or spell *lose* as *loose*. Misusing a common word marks a writer as careless, so a dictionary habit pays off for checking on items like these.

Fingerprints on writing. A genius of the English language is its wonderful flexibility. If everything were governed by rigid rules then everybody's writings would be alike. But they are not. Writers leave their individual fingerprints by the way they handle the language.

A Shakespeare scholar, Don Foster, invented a system of reading author fingerprints. A poem signed W. S. had long been a mystery. Was it by William Shakespeare or not? Foster wrote his dissertation to show that based on word usage and sentence formats it was indeed Shakespeare. But scholars are slow to change their minds. At Shakespeare conventions Foster's theory made no headway until after he successfully identified the authors in some cases that were highly visible in the news—the anonymous author of *The Color Purple* and some serial killers. Now the professors believe he is right about Shakespeare's poem.

Did the apostle Paul write the letter to the Hebrews or not? A study of his writing fingerprints might answer that. For instance, one mannerism we can detect even in English (King James) is a repeated use of *again* or *and again* followed by a comma, as though to say "I tell you again." This usage occurs in about the same percentage in all of Paul's letters. It never occurs in the letters of James, Peter, John, or Jude. Studies of parallelism and other features cannot be done easily by computer, but a good linguistic detective could no doubt settle the authorship question conclusively.

No matter how many word lists you had to study in school, the body of words you take for your own is unique. It matches no one else's body of words. The way you arrange the words in phrases and sentences also is unique. Your mannerisms and tone and other features are uniquely yours. You leave fingerprints every time you write, prints of your thoughts and of the way you express them.

Let's close here with some fingerprints of Winston Churchill about learning English.

> I continued in this unpretentious situation for nearly a year. However, by being so long in the lowest form [seventh grade equivalent] I gained an immense advantage over the cleverer boys. They all went on to learn Latin and Greek and splendid things like that. But I was taught English . . . As I remained in the Third Fourth [sophomore] . . . three times as long as anyone else, I had three times as much of it. I learned it thoroughly. Thus I got into my bones the essential structure of the British sentence— which is a noble thing. And when in after years my school-fellows who had won prizes and distinction for writing such beautiful Latin poetry and pithy Greek epigrams had to come down again to common English, to earn their living or make their way, I did not feel myself at any disadvantage. Naturally I am biased in favor of boys learning English. I would make them all learn English: and then I would let the clever ones learn Latin as an honour, and Greek as a treat. But the only thing I would whip them for is not knowing English. I would whip them hard for that.

4. How English Language Came to Us

Most linguists at one time believed that languages evolved separately in different areas of the world. That follows from their evolutionary view of history. But as linguistic researches progressed, many came to see that no, all languages must have had a common ancestor. They haven't yet named that original ancestor and they're having trouble fitting some languages into the chain of descent, but the big picture of languages branching from a single tree remains the major view.

Bible believers all along knew that before Babel there was one grandmother language, probably the original Hebrew. Linguists have not traced back to the pre-Babel language. But they do trace back to three major branches—Hamitic, Semitic (formerly Shemitic), and Indo-European (formerly Japhetic). Some writers express pleasure that the linguistic world grew smart enough to drop the "mythical" name Japhetic and, unfortunately, we are stuck with the new name.

On our chart we show parts of that Indo-European branch. The second generation consists of two sisters separated by the way they made certain sounds, especially k. The cut-off sister on the right would lead to a number of Slavic, Iranian, and Indic languages—all in the East. Sanskrit appeared over there, too. Sanskrit rivaled ancient Greek and Latin, and we have excellent grammars of that language. One book says that when the Greeks were indulging in reckless speculations about language (fourth century BC) a man named Panini "wrote a grammar of Sanskrit which to this day holds the admiration of linguistic scholars."

Others after Panini put "much of the grammatical writings of the Greeks and Romans to shame."[i]

On the continent. From the sister on the left of the chart, we show three descendants in the next generation—Hellenic, Germanic, and Italic. This is closer now to the languages we are familiar with today. Hellenic was a grandmother to Greek, Italic a grandmother to Latin, and Germanic a grandmother to English. These started off as first cousins, we might say, but their descendants became second and third cousins and eventually quite distant cousins with less resemblance to one another.

From the Germanic line in northern Europe came the story of Beowulf. In that time, Denmark was being plagued with a murderous monster called Grendel. Prince Beowulf lived on a Swedish island nearby, and he and his warriors were skilled at killing those dinosaur monsters, so they sailed to Denmark to help. That is where the story happened.[ii]

Literature books usually call this story the first novel in English, but it more likely is true history, though no doubt embellished. The story gives evidence that the people knew of creation, of Adam and Eve, and other early people, as was true in many parts of the world. But they knew no later Bible history. This dates the writing to pre-Christian times for those Germanic tribes in northern Europe. The language had gained a few church words such as *pope* and *archbishop* from Germanic invasions into southern Europe. But the northern people seemed to know nothing else of Christianity. We now call their language Old English, the language that *Beowulf* was written in.

In England. For centuries both before and after Beowulf, Germanic tribes, including the Angles and Saxons, were invading England. There they encountered mostly the Celtic language. The Roman Empire had been master of the country for a few

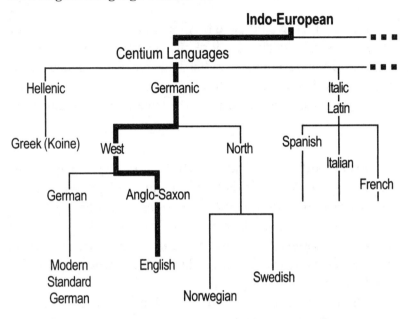

centuries, but they never succeeded in making the native Celts learn Latin. When the Romans withdrew, about Beowulf's time, the language left with them.

Germanic tribes from the continent outnumbered and conquered the Celts (Britons), who fled to Wales where their language survives today. Some fled to northern France and founded Brittany from where they later helped to invade England. But that's getting ahead of the story. It is hard to keep all the peoples straight in English history since the Welsh are Britons, the Picts are Scots, the Celts are Welsh, and on and on.

To skip all that, the native Celtic languages either died out or moved, and the invading Germanic languages conquered. Saint Augustine arrived to convert the tribes to Christianity—a different Augustine than the author of *City of God*. He conducted religious rituals in Latin, and nobody understood the Latin. King Alfred wrote that there were a multitude of God's servants but they had little knowledge of the books because they were not written in their language.

No one then would have predicted the future of the minor Anglo-Saxon language. But looking backward now, we see that those times of developing English had great significance for future general history and for future language history. The unpredicted happened and English became the most widely used language in the world.

French influence. The year 1066 is to English school children what the year 1776 is to American children. William the Conqueror crossed the channel from Normandy in northern France and became king of all England. (His neighbor Britons helped with the invasion.) That was a major language event, as well as political event, because it infused French elements into the English language.

The French even then led in fashion and cooking, so the English added words like *boil, fry, roast*, and words like *apparel, costume*, and *garment.* They no longer ate sheep, but the French mutton; and instead of cow and calf they ate beef and veal. After the conquest, French Normans were the elite in society, the rich and powerful, and an English trait was to emulate them. Do we see the same trait today in the high interest that people show in the doings of royalty and other celebrities? The elite classes held power in law and military matters and they had more leisure (a French word) for arts, so in those many fields they had words hitherto unknown to the English, and the English began importing them.

The first couple of generations did not borrow words, but in time numerous French words became a part of English. People Anglicized them by adding *ing* to French verbs or apostrophe *s* to French nouns. Or sometimes they used their own words, like *shepherd*, and added the French ending *ess*. A three-way hybrid is *trusteeship. Trust* was Scandinavian (north Germanic), *ee* a French ending, and *ship* an Old English ending. Through all these changes, the English language dominated; England never became a French-speaking nation. The reverse happened—French invaders assimilated into English.

Latin influence. The next historical event for English language was the Renaissance, which came to England through Italy and France. This was a revival of the learning of ancient Greeks and Romans, who had left more writings than Germanic nations had. Puritans and others strongly objected to this humanist and pagan education, but in certain centuries the educated people became so steeped in Latin that they lost the habit of looking to their own language for new expressions. They drew from Latin instead. The new Latin-imported words came mostly through French so it is often impossible to separate whether the word origins are Latin or French. Linguists who have tried to count the number of these French-Latin words now in our language vary in their estimates from about five percent to fifteen percent. Again, the English often added their own inflections and pronunciations and even changed the shades of meanings of the Latin loan-words. In modern times we still see this borrowing, particularly in science and technology where we often need to coin new words. These newly coined words spread throughout the world because English is now the international science language.

Borrowing was not always so happy. English had the words *cold, cool, chill, chilly, icy,* and *frosty,* so they did not need the Latin word *frigid.* Shakespeare, Milton, Pope and other poets, and the King James Bible do not contain *frigid.* It became pretentious or snobbish to use Latin words when perfectly good English words would do, and writers discussed this. Dickens satirized the practice. Tennyson was proud that he used fewer Latin words in *Idylls of the King* than other poets used. A writer in "The Times" in England wrote in 1890 that "the worst and most debased kinds of English styles are those which ape Latiny."

Otto Jespersen, the greatest twentieth century linguist, called the Latin infection a malady that lingers on especially in the half-educated.[iii]

Throughout Old English history, the language contained plenty of words, as is always true of people who live close to the earth. From Alaskan islanders I learned *dory*, *skiff*, *dinghy*, and probably a few more now forgotten words to add to my boat vocabulary. *Beowulf* has eleven words for boat, seventeen for sea, twelve for battle, and thirty-six for prince. And this poem did not exhaust the words for boat; other old poems used sixteen more. Linguists who see that wealth of vocabulary argue, like Jespersen, that English would have been better off if writers had searched their native language for needed words instead of succumbing to the habit of borrowing.

Among the unhappy results of borrowing is that the genius of English dried up in some ways. For instance, English has many endings by which to make adjectives from nouns—wood*en*, book*ish*, salt*y*, father*ly*, child*like*, trouble*some*, sin*ful*. Yet the Latin-steeped writers did not say fatherly but paternal, not watery but aquatic, and so on. *Oral* became the adjective that goes with mouth, *ocular* with eye, and *solar* with sun. This discordant clashing of two systems permeates most areas of English now. English would be easier to learn if it had developed along its own lines. It would be more "democratic." That is, all classes of people would communicate freely, instead of a Latin-educated class separating themselves with words unnatural to English.

We now inherit the dissonant mixture and we inherit the same old language battles that people fought centuries ago. Can we use *that* for a relative pronoun or must we stick with *who* and *which*? Can we say "the age I live in" or must we say "the age in which I live"? Should a reporter tell about the great fire or about the disastrous conflagration?

Professional writers telling how to achieve smooth,

understandable writing lean toward the natural English choices, while many schoolbook grammars continue to push toward Latin-style grammar. Among some groups there is also a push toward everybody studying the Latin language itself, though other education leaders advise studying a modern language instead.

That is our position now in history. Where will English language be in one hundred years? If Bible believers are right, we may well be back to the original "pure language."[iv] In the meantime, we writers should make the best use we can of the incredible English language.

---

[i] Thomas Pyles, *The Origins and Development of the English Language,* 1964 (New York: Harcourt, Brace) p 83. This is a good book for more information on language history.

[ii] Details vary in different sources, but the best researched and most accurate history is given in the interesting chapter 11 of *After the Flood* by Bill Cooper, 1995 (England: New Wine Press).

[iii] Otto Jespersen, *Growth and Structure of the English Language,* 1948 (New York: Macmillan) p 134. This is one of several good books on language by this linguist.

[iv] Zephaniah 3:9.

Glossary of Grammar Terms

absolute   an adjective or adverb that cannot logically have a comparative degree, as *unique* cannot be said to be *more unique*

abstract word   refers to something general rather than to something specific

active voice   verb form used when the subject is doing something

adjective   a word that modifies a noun or pronoun

adverb   a word that modifies a verb, adjective, or other adverb

agreement   showing whether subject and verb or pronoun and antecedent agree as to number (singular or plural) and gender (masculine, feminine, neuter)

ambiguous   unclear either by word choice or by sentence format

antecedent   the word or group of words that a pronoun stands for

case   can be subjective, nominative, objective, or possessive; shown on nouns or pronouns by their word form or by position in a sentence

clause   a group of words that contain both a subject and predicate

close comma system   uses practically all the commas that are allowed by grammar rules

command   a type of sentence called imperative; directed *to* someone: Go easy with that.

complement   word or words that complete the sense of a verb; sometimes an object of the verb, sometimes related to the subject; not the same as *compliment*

compound sentence   contains two or more clauses

concrete   tangible, specific, not generalized

conjunction   a word that joins words, phrases, clauses, or sentences

conjunctive adverb   connects clauses as does a conjunction, and shows relationship between them as does an adverb

connotation   the meaning that a word suggests, not its denotation as in a dictionary

denotation   the specific meaning of a word as given in a dictionary

exclamation mark   used after an emphatic utterance or sometimes to indicate irony

expository writing   explains or analyzes a subject, not emotional

gender   form of pronouns to specify sex—masculine, feminine, or neuter

grammar   the formal features of the words and sentences of the language, including word inflections and sentence syntax

inflections   endings of words that show plural, tense, person, or possession; with modifiers they show comparison (fast, faster, fastest)

jargon originally referred to the vocabulary of a specific profession; now also means ambiguous or pretentious words that weaken the meaning

irregular verb a verb that does not form past tense in the standard way of adding *d* or *ed*

linkage writing techniques that produce a logical flow of ideas; not the same as the grammatical terms of "linking verbs" or "linking sentences"

linking sentence contains a linking verb that connects the subject with its complement

linking verb all forms of *to be* and a few other verbs such as *seem, feel, look, sound*

metaphor a figure of speech by which one thing is made to be like another in some of its characteristics

modifier word or group of words used to describe, limit, or qualify another word or group of words

nominative the case of a word used for the subject or complement of a verb; only pronouns change form for this (*he* and *she* are nominative)

number refers to singular and plural

noun the part of speech that names something—a person, place, thing, idea, or quality

noun phrase a group of words that can act as a noun in a sentence

object the word (or phrase or clause) that receives the action of an active verb

objective the case of a word used for the object of a verb or preposition; only pronouns change form for cases (*him* and *her* are objective case)

open comma system   uses only what commas are needed for clarity and smooth reading plus those required by universal consensus

paragraph   a few sentences (usually) that form a coherent unit of meaning; begins with indentation

parallelism   the form that puts equal ideas into the same type of sentence construction

parenthetical   an explanatory or qualifying remark usually enclosed by parentheses or by commas

passive voice   verb form used when the subject is having something done to it

person   the form of a verb or pronoun that shows whether it refers to the person speaking, the person spoken to, or the person spoken of (called first, second, and third person)

phrase   a group of words without a subject and verb that can be used together as a noun, adjective, or adverb

plural   refers to more than one; nouns, pronouns, and verbs change form for plural

possessive case   a noun or pronoun form that shows belonging to; apostrophe *s* added to nouns; and pronoun form changed, for example to *his*, *mine*, and *theirs*

predicate   the verb with any modifiers that go with it

prefix   element added before a word root: *un*zip, *re*write

preposition   a word that relates a noun or pronoun to another word in the sentence; examples are *up*, *to*, *of*, *over*, and *on*

pronoun   a word that takes the place of a noun; types include personal, relative, interrogative, demonstrative, indefinite, and reflexive

regular verb   a verb that adds *d* or *ed* for past tense

relative pronoun   relates one part of a sentence to another part: who, which, that

sentence   definition in the *Oxford English Dictionary* is the word or words that extend from one full stop to another —stops marked by period, question mark, or exclamation mark

singular   word form that refers to only one

standard English   the most widely used forms approved by educated English-speaking people; has levels of formal and informal

subject   a word, phrase, or clause in a sentence about which the verb makes a statement

subjective   form of a pronoun that shows it is a subject (*he* not *him*)

substantive   any word or group of words that acts as a noun in a sentence

suffix   element added after the root of a word: mak*ing*, understand*able*

syntax   the arrangement of words in a phrase or sentence

tense   verb forms that show whether the action is past or present; shows future by adding *will* to the verb

transitive verb   a verb that can take a direct object

verb   a word that asserts action, state, or being

Index

Index   *83*

Other books by Ruth Beechick

Adam and His Kin

Dr. Beechick's Homeschool Answer Book

Genesis: Finding Our Roots

Heart & Mind: What the Bible Says About Learning

Language and Thinking for Young Children

The Cabin and the Ice Palace

The Language Wars: and Other Writings
         for Homeschoolers

The Three R's: Grades K-3

You Can Teach Your Child Successfully:
         Grades 4-8 (hardback)

You Can Teach Your Child Successfully:
         Grades 4-8 (paperback)

World History Made Simple: Matching History
         with the Bible